I0423518

Strong Marriage Happy Life

The Core Principles Of A Successful Marriage And How to Make Your Marriage Work

Table of Contents

Introduction

I want to thank you and congratulate you for purchasing the book *Strong Marriage, Happy Life: The Core Principles of a Successful Marriage and How to Make Your Marriage Work*.

This book contains proven steps and strategies on how to make your marriage work by applying the principles of successful marriages.

If you're about to get married, if you've just gotten married, or if you've been in a marriage that seems to be going nowhere, then this book is for you. Knowing how to make your marriage work is an important aspect of happily living the rest of your adult life. *Strong Marriage Happy Life* teaches you the core principles of successful marriages and how you can implement them to make your marriage work. In other words, this book teaches you the secrets to having a happy married life. It's exactly how our favorite fairy tales end: you and your spouse living happily ever after.

Thanks again for purchasing this book. I hope you enjoy it!

Chapter 1: Nurturing Love

Love is the most important aspect of marriage to many people. Most of us decide whether or not to get married more on the basis of our feelings of "love" than of any other aspect of our relationship, and we evaluate the success of our marriage on the basis of those feelings more than anything else. A surprising feature of the "love" aspect of marriage is that, even in these times of rapid social change and innovative lifestyles, it is an aspect that most people do not want to change. This very important part of marriage is, however, difficult to study because love means very different things to different people and it is an extremely difficult experience to define.

In this chapter we will begin with defining love. Then we will discuss what affects the level of the love feelings in a relationship. In the last section, we will discuss ways to apply these love-related principles in marriage.

Defining Love

It seems useful to begin by identifying some of the ways by which the term *love* has been defined. The ancient Greeks used two different words to describe two different types of love. *Agape* was the term for an unselfish, brotherly, or spiritual type of love which did not include sexual implications. *Eros* was the term for a more sensuous, sexually-driven love.

The term love used in this book refers to a particular type of emotional feeling that one person has about another person. There is first the condition of "liking" another person. Here we have kindly, favorable, or friendly feelings toward the other person, or what psychologists call positive *affect*. Love, however, is a more intense positive affective experience than just liking another person, and there is no other word in the English language to describe that experience than the word *love.*

When love is defined in this way, it does not include any behaviors or acts. It is an emotional experience that is felt rather than an action that is performed. Of course, when we experience intense love feelings, we are highly motivated, and this active arousal leads to all sorts of behaviors. Sometimes we do things that we are later glad we did, and other times we do things we later feel embarrassed or sorry about, but these behaviors are *effects* of love and not the emotion itself. The emotion of love, as it is defined here, also usually leads to having a number of other emotional and intellectual experiences, such as caring very much about other persons, being concerned about their welfare, trying to do things for them that they appreciate, and wanting to be around them, but these too are effects of love.

Hopefully, the definition used here is reasonably clear. While some might prefer a broader definition, this description makes it possible to identify some general principles about love that can be used to make marriage work.

A Simple Principle

The very general principle about love is called the Profit Principle. It is simply that *the more a person provides a pleasurable or rewarding experience for you, the more intense your "love" feelings will be toward that person.*

Implementing the Profit Principle

The profit principle is so encompassing and abstract. It becomes difficult to identify ways to apply it. Because of this, several more specific principles are deduced from this very general principle.

THE INTERACTION PRINCIPLE:

> When the interaction between two individuals is profitable, the more they interact the stronger their love for each other will be. Conversely, the less they interact, the less intense their love.

Finding Ways to Interact

Get together with a small group of friends and make a list of specific activities that couples can do together without children. In each of the following categories, try to come up with at least five or six activities you think are pleasant in addition to the examples given to get you started.

- o Recreational interaction (take a quiet walk together, have dinner at home alone—by candlelight, join a dancing club, get season tickets to the symphony)

- o Learning activities (learn a language through records, take an adult education class together, learn a new sport together)

- o Communicating (look at your partner while speaking and listening, put little notes in your partner's pocket, write a poem for your partner)

- o Doing different things while near each other (one shines shoes in the kitchen while the other does dishes)

- o Working together (wash car or dishes together, work in the yard together, redecorate a room together)

- o Expressing affection (seat wife at a dinner table, turn down blankets and lay out slippers and robe for spouse, hold hands while window-shopping, touch seated spouse when passing him or her)

Increasing the Profit in Interaction (Changing the Quality of Interaction):

1. List three regularly occurring interactions on your relationship in which you might be able to increase the profit. Using a piece of paper in the following manner is often useful:

   i. *Eating dinner*. By the time I have prepared a meal and sat down, I am too tired and flustered to be responsive company.

   ii. *Saying good morning*. I'm often grouchy and slow to wake up.

   iii. *Visiting in-laws:* No particular loss or reward.

2. Choose any of the items you listed, and with your partner, think of some way to reduce or

eliminate its costly aspects or to increase its rewards.

3. Implement your plan.

4. After a reasonable time, determine whether or not you actually increased the profit. If so, describe any effects this had on your feelings in the relationship. If not, what probably hindered you?

THE SENSE OF IMPORTANCE PRINCIPLE:

> The more important an individual feels he or she is to someone else, the stronger the love feelings will be toward the other person. Conversely, the less important he or she feels, the less intense the love feelings toward the other person.

Evaluating the Importance of Someone as a Person

Determine how frequently you think the following ten events occur. Rate their frequency this way: N—never occurs; O—occasionally occurs; F—frequently occurs; A—always occurs.

1. We attentively listen to the other person.

2. We express appreciation or approval for something the other person has done.

3. We go out of our way to greet the other person when we meet or say goodbye when we separate.

4. We plan to take into account the other person's suggestions.

5. We are concerned about the other person's feelings.

6. The other person expresses a wish or desire, and we ignore it.

7. The other person states an opinion, and we treat it as unimportant.

8. We are in a situation in which the other person deserves an apology, but we don't give it.

9. The other person wants help, but we are too busy.

10. We keep the other person waiting.

Get the other person to rate how frequently these ten events occur, and compare your evaluations.

If your first five answers tend to be closer to "A" and your second five tend toward "N," this indicates a sense of importance. If the other person perceives you as showing less importance than you perceive, this may indicate that his or her actual importance to you is less than you think.

THE EMOTIONAL HELP PRINCIPLE:

> The more help a person provides in times of emotional distress, the greater the intensity of the love feelings toward this person will be. Conversely, the less help a person provides, the less intense the love feelings.

Determining Your Sources of Emotional Help

1. Have a relaxed, uninterrupted conversation with someone with whom you have a close relationship. This conversation may take considerable time, so select a time when you do not have other obligations.

2. Everyone occasionally experience different combinations of sadness, discouragement, loneliness and depression. Discuss what you do when you experience these emotions. Who do you find helpful? Determine whether it is friends, parents, children, spouse, roommates, or someone else. Try to determine how different people help in different ways — if they help at all.

3. Emotional help is usually needed in a time of crisis, such as severe illness, a serious accident, or death. Talk about what you do at such times. To whom can you turn for encouragement and support? Again, try to determine how different individuals help in different ways.

4. Evaluate how you feel about your interpersonal resources for different types of emotional help. Are you satisfied with these relationships, or are there ways to improve them? Is your spouse of too little help or does he or she help too much?

5. If you would like to make changes in your sources of emotional help, try to identify specific things that could be done to affect such changes.

With these three specific principles and one general principle, you are now a few steps closer to a successful marriage. In the chapters to come, you will discover many other principles of making marriages work and stand the test of time.

Chapter 2: Keeping the Ties

The ties that keep two or more people together in a relationship can also be called a *bond.* A number of other concepts in the social sciences have virtually the same meaning, and some of them are: *cohesion, attachment, connectedness, solidarity, interdependence* and *attraction.*

There are two reasons why relationship ties are important enough to have an entire chapter devoted to them. First, most couples in contemporary society want to have relatively strong ties to each other in their marriage, so having these ties is vital to the marriage's success. It is something that most couples feel strongly about.

Second, ties are important in marriage because people sometimes want to change the strength of the ties they have with their partner. During courtship, for example, most people want to increase their ties to the other person, and they use such things as songs, promises, pins, rings, and affection to strengthen those ties. At other stages of the family life cycle people want to decrease their ties to others. An example of this is that all marital relationships are eventually broken by death or divorce, and when this occurs most people want to decrease their attachment to the other person. Therefore, the main goal in this chapter is to discuss principles that can be used to increase or decrease the ties in a marital relationship.

The Principles About Ties

There are three principles that identify factors that influence the ties in a relationship. Hopefully, knowledge of these principles, coupled with the skills to implement them, will increase your control of the connectedness in your marriage. Very strong ties, however, are not necessarily an optimal goal. It is your value system, with its ideas about the importance, functions and style of marriage, that will determine the strength of the ties you want. Based on this, you can use these principles help you attain your goals.

THE SHARED EXPERIENCE PRINCIPLE:

> The amount of shared experiences a couple has influences the strength of their ties, and this is a positive, linear experience.

Increasing Shared Experience

1. Each day for a week deliberately plan to do one of the following two things:

a. Engage in some pleasant activity that you have not previously done together. Do it as a pair only—no one else with you. This can involve such ordinary things as one helping the other with some chore, engaging in a new leisure activity such as miniature golf or billiards, visiting a museum, etc.

b. Discuss some previous experience in your life or lives that you have not talked about before. Try to select something that is or was fairly important, and remember that the object is for the other person, in a sense, to share the experience with you.

2. At the end of the week, both of you try to identify whether there are differences in the bonds in your relationship.

Decreasing Shared Experience

1. Carry a notebook or a piece of paper for one week—in your pocket, purse, etc.

2. During the week, try to identify experiences you are now having or have had in the past that you will not share with the other person. Number these experiences, and describe them briefly in writing.

3. At the end of the week, review the list of experiences and evaluate how much this exercise has increased your independence from the other person.

THE INCOMPLETE ACTION PRINCIPLE:

The amount of investment in incomplete action influences the ties in a relationship.

Incomplete action occurs when a couple has already invested time, energy, thought, or planning in something that requires both of them for its completion.

Increasing Incomplete Action

1. Think up several things to do that (a) cannot be done unless both members of the couple are involved in them and (b) will take a relatively long period of time. These could

include such diverse activities as joining a bridge or dance club, paying musical duets, working on a committee, collaborating on something like writing or decorating, planning now what to do next on year's vacation, starting a new tradition like going out on a certain date each month, or having breakfast in bed every rainy Saturday. Be creative on thinking up novel or exotic things.

2. Select one of the ideas in step #1 and implement it. After you have become involved in it enough to have really invested yourself in the experience, take some time to evaluate whether you have experienced any change in the connectedness in the relationship.

THE SUPPORT PRINCIPLE:

The amount of support in a relationship influences the strength of the ties in that relationship.

Evaluating and increasing support

1. Find the time for a 30 minute discussion about supportiveness in the relationship.

2. Identify five recent situations in which you were supportive. List these on a piece of paper. If you are interested in increasing the supportiveness of the other person, also complete steps 2, 3, and 4 for that person. Some situations in which supportiveness may have occurred are:

a. When one person did something to make the other feel better about herself or himself.

b. When one person was feeling low or discouraged and needed someone to turn to.

c. When one person encouraged the other.

d. When one person showed confidence in the other.

e. When one person did something that showed he or she cared about the other.

3. Identify three situations in which you could have been more supportive than you were. List these on a piece of paper.

4. Select one way in which you could be more supportive, and develop an *action plan.* You may want to select one of the behaviors mentioned in step #3, or you may want to select some other behavior.

Your Action Plan

1. Ask yourself: what do you want to change?

... Is it to do something less often?

... Is it to do something more often?

... Is it to start doing something?

... Is it to stop doing something?

2. Would you be committed to make the change? If yes, to what degree?

... In regard to the action plan, will you be faithful to your actions?

...Will you be accountable for what you do? (No passing of responsibility to situational circumstances or to another person)

3. What exactly is your action plan?

... Is it an observable behavior? (One that is small and manageable.)

...When do you plan to do it?

... How often do you plan to do it?

... State it as: *who* will do *what* for *whom* and *when* you will finish it.

4. Follow-up.

Record the results of your action plan. Remember that results near to your expectations are successes, not failures. Your perseverance may lead to total success.

After completing your action plan, describe the results.

In this chapter, we have mentioned three factors that influence the ties in marital relationships. In the next chapter, you will be introduced to some more principles useful for attaining a happy marriage.

Chapter 3: Sexuality in Marriage

The sexual relationship is an important part of the total marital experience for a number of reasons. A pleasant sexual relationship can create meaning and commitment and foster several different types of interpersonal intimacy. It can also provide physical sensory pleasure so unique and intense that it defies verbal description, and it can be the source of emotional and interpersonal pleasures that are among the most rewarding experiences known. In this chapter, you will learn two principles that can help you and your spouse increase your chances of experiencing those pleasures and benefits.

The Body's Most Sexually Sensitive Parts

The Male's Sexually Sensitive Parts

The penis is the man's reproductive and sexual organ. During periods of sexual excitement it increases in size and becomes erect. When the penis is fully erect it projects outward from the body and typically curves upward. The average length of an erect penis is usually about six inches, the average diameter about an inch and a half. Erection is caused by constrictions in the blood vessels that lead from the penis. These constrictions cause the spongy tissue in the penis to become filled with blood and hence to become larger and fairly firm. The "head" of the penis has a very high concentration of sexually active nerve endings, and it is stimulation of these nerve endings that gradually increases the male's sexual excitement to its peak and brings about the ejaculation of semen. The crown-like ridge at the back of the head usually has the highest concentration of nerve endings.

The Female's Sexually Sensitive Parts

The part of the female into which the penis is inserted during sexual intercourse is known as the *vagina*. When a woman is sexually excited, the vaginal cavity becomes considerably longer and larger in diameter, and the vaginal tissues become sufficiently elastic to permit a normal vagina to accommodate an erect penis. If the woman is not sexually aroused, however, and she is apprehensive or tense when intercourse is attempted, the tissue around the vagina contracts and the size of the vagina reduces considerably. Under those circumstances, attempts to insert the penis into the vagina are usually painful.

Since parts of the vagina have sensitive nerve endings, they provide sexual excitement when they are simulated. The walls of the vagina have relatively few nerve endings, but the tissue surrounding the vaginal opening, called *lips* or *labia,* are more sensitive. The labia minora, or inner lips, especially the parts close to the vaginal opening, are one of the most sensitive areas for most women. There is also a high concentration of nerve endings in the clitoris. The clitoris is a small projection in the front part of the external genitalia. It has a shaft and head, and the head is so sensitive that most women find it uncomfortable if the head is manipulated very much directly. However, indirect simulation of the clitoris by stimulating the shaft is usually very sexually exciting, and the female usually achieves orgasm, or sexual climax, through the combined stimulation of the labia minora and clitoris that occurs with the joint movement of the male and female during intercourse. It is possible for many women to experience an orgasm by stimulating only one of these areas, but this is less common. It is also possible for women to achieve an orgasm through simulation of other parts of the body, such as the nipples, or through fantasy, but these conditions are very rare.

The Sexual Response Cycle

There is a predictable cycle in the way most people respond to sexual stimulation, and an awareness of this cycle can facilitate the sexual compatibility and satisfaction. On the other hand, a lack of awareness of how you or your spouse responds to sexual excitement can lead to endless frustration, dissatisfaction and bitterness.

The cycle consists of the excitement phase, the plateau phase, the orgasmic phase, and the resolution phase. The first is the period when an individual becomes increasingly sexually excited. The second is the stage in which an individual who is highly aroused sexually can remain for sometime without becoming appreciably more or less sexually excited. The third is usually the shortest of the four stages, as it seldom lasts more than a few seconds. It is the period when the peak of sexual excitement occurs. The last is the period of gradual decrease in sexual excitement.

Women typically can attain multiple orgasms before entering the resolution phase. The male tends to move immediately into the resolution phase. Even though the average duration of an orgasm is usually three to four seconds, women can occasionally experience much longer climaxes—up to 40 - 60 seconds.

Principles About Sexuality

THE SPECTATOR PRINCIPLE:

> Assuming a spectator role during sexual intercourse tends to interfere with sexual adequacy.

When the persons are spectators this means that they are conscious of themselves as participants and are concerned about "what" they are doing, "how" they are doing it, and what their reactions are. They are observers of themselves, of their partners, and of what is occurring. This contrasts with simply allowing natural feelings, inclinations, and actions to occur without being conscious of them or of oneself.

One way to use this principle would be for a couple to discuss whether either of them tends to assume a spectator role during highly erotic sexual activity. If one or the other does, try to identify what he or she could do to change this tendency.

THE PLEASURIZING PRINCIPLE:

> The greater the sensory "pleasuring" in a relationship — exclusive of the sexual intercourse — the greater the sexual adequacy.

Recognizing Pleasuring

1. It is possible to provide and receive sensory pleasure that is not specifically related to sexual intercourse, and this step is an attempt to identify how much this happens in a relationship. Evaluate each of the following items according to how often it occurs in your relationship: Never, very seldom, occasionally, or frequently.

a. Gently touch the skin of the other person in an affectionate caressing manner.

b. Kiss in a variety of different ways, such as on the lips and other areas, short and long, gentle and firm, on intimate occasions and at other times, alone and around others, etc.

c. "Say something" by delicately touching.

d. Create a feeling in the other person by softly touching ears, neck, closed eyes, cheeks, etc.

e. Pause and savor a feeling one has for a long, sensing time.

f. Deeply enjoy sensations of different parts of one's body, such as hands, toes, skin.

g. Completely and totally relax and enjoy whatever sensations occur.

7 Myths and Truths About Sex

There are a large number of beliefs, traditions, and opinions about various aspects of sex that persist even though there is growing evidence that many of them are not true. These myths frequently interfere with pleasant, satisfying sexual interaction.

1. Myth: Males respond more quickly to sexual stimuli than do females.

Fact: The walls of vagina begin secreting lubricants within 10–15 seconds of effective sexual stimulation.

2. Myth: Reaching an orgasm simultaneously is best.

Fact: When simultaneous orgasm occurs, the husband moves immediately to the resolution phase and his subsequent loss of interest and erection may prevent the wife from attaining subsequent orgasms during the intercourse if she wishes to.

3. Myth: Women are not completely satisfied with their sex life if they fail to achieve orgasm at least a majority of the times they engage in intercourse.

Fact: Many wives report that they are highly satisfied with their sex life even though they seldom or never experience orgasm.

4. Myth: Women cannot participate or are not interested in participating in intercourse after the menopause.

Fact: After the menopause, the tissues in the genital region tend to have less tone and elasticity, but the female sexual organs continue to function effectively when there is an appropriate interpersonal relationship and normal sexual stimulation.

5. Myth: People are able to have certain number of sexual experiences, and when those are used up, their sexual activity is over.

Fact: People establish a pattern of participation in sexual activity when they are young, and this pattern tends continue throughout their lives.

6. Myth: Both highly frequent sexual participation and sexual abstinence is harmful.

Fact: No lasting physiological or psychological effects can be attributed to either high or low participation in sexual activity. Also, sexual desire is increased when couples abstain from intercourse for short periods of time. There is no evidence that either very frequent or very infrequent sexual activity has any systematic harmful effects—physically, mentally, or emotionally.

7. Myth: The size of the penis and foreskin makes a difference in sexual gratification.

Fact: There is almost no correlation between body size and penile size, and very often small men have a large penis and large men have a small penis. The size of penis does not affect sexual gratification simply because the vaginal walls have an extremely low concentration of nerve endings.

Familiarizing yourself with the information provided in this chapter will help you have a satisfying sexual life. A satisfying sexual life plays an important role in the success of your marriage.

Chapter 4: Coping with Stress

It is possible to create a pleasant, rewarding marriage and family life, but even in ideal relationships, difficult and stressful situations are inevitable. Some stressful situations are sudden and unexpected, such as an accident that seriously injures a member of the family or the birth of a child who is mentally disabled or physically deformed. Other stressful situations, such as bereavement, are as unavoidable as the changing of the seasons.

Many of us are well into adulthood before we encounter situations that teach us such things as the inevitability of tragedy or the effects that stress has on intimate relationships. The result is that when we eventually learn how extensive stressful events really are, this can be a fairly shocking experience in itself. In this chapter you will learn new principles to help you cope with stress.

Principles of Avoiding and Recovering from Crises

THE ADAPTABILITY PRINCIPLE:

> The greater the adaptability of a family, the less vulnerable it is to stress, and vice versa.

It is relatively easy to find illustrations of this principle in family life situations. One obvious example is a situation in which a family's primary source of income is lost through an accident, illness or economic depression. Families that rigidly adhere to a particular set of beliefs, such as the belief that the wife should not work or that the family should not accept help from private or public sources, will usually find this event to be a very serious crisis. On the other hand, more adaptable families will feel less threatened in the same situation.

Assessing Adaptability

1. Think of the view, idea, opinion, value, etc. about marital and family life which you are least willing to change. Write it down.

2. Think of the view, etc. about which you are least adaptable, and continue doing this until you have a list of the eight to ten areas of low adaptability.

3. Think of eight to ten views, etc. about marital or family life that you would be willing to change, and make a second list.

4. If possible, do this with your partner. Compare the lists and then discuss how each of you feels emotionally about the two lists.

5. The following list will get you started.

a. I want to have a considerable time to myself.

b. I want a spouse who is very sexually responsive.

c. I want to have a career outside the home.

d. Sex should (should not) be confined to marriage.

e. Men and women should be completely equal.

f. My children must be very obedient to their parents.

g. I want a very affectionate marital relationship.

h. I want to engage in outside sports.

i. I want to spend a great deal of time reading.

Increasing Adaptability

1. Make a list of five to ten opinions you have about the way things ought to be in marriage. (If you did the previous exercise you can use the list you made there.)

2. Identify which of these opinions you tend to value intrinsically (as ends or goals in themselves) and which you value mostly because they are instrumental in helping you attain some other ends or goals. Examples of instrumental opinions might be:

a. My wife should not work... not because working is bad, but because the children need care, and if she worked she couldn't care for them.

b. My husband (or wife) should be the one to initiate our lovemaking... not because I want him (or her) to take the initiative but because this will show that he (she) desires me.

3. Pick the one instrumental opinion you feel least strongly about.

4. Talk to some intimate acquaintance (spouse, good friend, etc.) about your opinion. The aim

of your discussion is to find several ways in which your goal or end might be accomplished other than the way you started with. This should help make you more adaptable than you were previously.

THE PRIOR ROLE LEARNING PRINCIPLE:

The amount of prior learning about a stressful event influences the vulnerability of families to that event and the ability to recover from that event.

This principle is illustrated by the fact that it is much easier to cope with the death of persons close to us the second time than the first time, as a great deal of learning seems to occur the first time an individual experiences bereavement. Two other examples that illustrate this principle are retirement and the birth of the first child.

Implement this principle by creating learning experiences that will prepare you for stressful situations you will probably experience in life. The following exercise should help you increase prior learning about stressful role changes.

Learning About Stressful Role Changes

1. Select a stressful role change, such as the illustrative examples mentioned above.

2. Consult with someone, such as a friend, neighbor, relative, or other acquaintance, who has experienced a change of this kind.

3. You will want to be tactful and delicate in discussing the experience, but see whether you can discuss such topics as:

a. Things the person found difficult about change.

b. Ways of behaving the person found useful in keeping the event from becoming a crisis.

c. What the person learned from the experience that he or she would use if the same situation were encountered again.

4. There is a great value in writing these types of things down, so you may benefit from making a list of these three things.

These two principles will help you cope with stress resulting from a potential crisis — a situation in which the marital system is so disrupted or disorganized that it cannot operate in its usual manner.

Chapter 5: Preparing for Parenthood

The transition into parenthood is one of the most complex and dramatic changes that most people ever make in their lives. Other major transitions, such as beginning to date, starting one's first job, graduating, marrying, and retiring, all involve some changes, but none compare to the process of becoming a parent. The coming of a child produces unalterable changes in the marital relationship, creates immense responsibilities for the welfare of a dependent human, rearranges most of the social and personal rhythms in a couple's life, and creates a variety of new obligations to friends, society, and relatives.

Planning About Parenthood

The most fundamental decision you and your partner have to make when it comes to parenthood is whether you should become parents at all. When you decide to become parents, you are faced with several other decisions: (1) when to have children, (2) the number of children you should have, and (3) desirable methods of controlling conception if you wish to do so.

Methods of Contraception

- *The pill*. Oral contraceptives, or the "pill," are now the most widely used medically prescribed method of birth control. It works by controlling the hormonal balance in the female so that conception is impossible.

- *Intrauterine devices (IUDs)*. An IUD is any plastic or metal device inserted into the uterus. Generally they work by altering the muscular activity of the uterus so that fertilized eggs do not become implanted.

- *The condom*. The condom is a thin sheath which fits over the erect penis. It controls the conception, because the seminal fluid ejaculated from the penis is confined to the condom rather than discharged into the vagina.

- *Rhythm.* The rhythm method of contraception refers to periodic abstinence from intercourse during the part of the menstrual cycle when conception is most likely.

- *Chemicals.* A variety of chemical substances are used to destroy sperm and thus prevent conception. They come in many forms, including aerosol spray cans, foaming tablets, creams, jellies, and suppositories.

- *Withdrawal.* In this method, the penis is removed from the vagina just prior to ejaculation. This prevents the seminal fluid from being expelled near the cervix.

- *Sterilization.* Sterilization can be performed on either the male or the female. In the male, this means tying and cutting the duct connected to the testicles, the part of male genitalia that produces sperm. In the female, this means cutting or clipping the fallopian tubes to interfere with the passage of the egg into the uterus.

Principles of Preparing for Parenthood

THE LEARNING ABOUT THE PARENT ROLE PRINCIPLE:

> The amount of prior learning about the parent role influences the ease of making the transition into parenthood.

This principle can be used in many ways to make the transition into parenthood easier, and most of us take advantage of it somewhat without ever realizing it. Routine activities, such as baby-tending and watching parents of infants, provide some insight into what the role of parenthood is like. Several activities can be done to consciously use this principle.

Take classes. Most communities have several organizations that teach courses on preparation for parenthood, and these classes can provide valuable prior learning. Frequently these classes are offered through such organizations as the YMCA or YWCA, a hospital, a medical clinic, a university extension or a continuing education center.

Practice parenthood. It is occasionally possible for a newly married couple to find an opportunity to become pseudo parents for a period of time. Most couples who have been married for several years would welcome the opportunity to have a responsible couple take care of their children for a weekend so that they can get away for vacation. This activity can provide you an opportunity to observe some aspects of parenthood and stimulate some discussion about your reactions to them.

Reading. There is a great deal of literature on infant care and parenthood, and it can provide some prior learning.

Talk to new parents. Most couples who have recently become parents love to talk endlessly about what they are experiencing, and you can take advantage of this to learn more about parenthood.

THE ROLE COMPATIBILITY PRINCIPLE:

> The amount of compatibility between the parent role and other roles influences the ease of the transition into the parent role.

Role compatibility refers to the degree to which the demands of an individual's various roles are compatible. For example, after the birth of their first child, many women find that if they continue the same work schedule, the demands of their career role interfere with their new role as a mother. In such situations sometimes the couple can change the nature of one of the roles so that the two roles are more compatible. For example, the wife may decide to work part-time or may change her work so that she works at home more. She may also change the way she plays the mother role by having someone else help her take care of the child.

If you can learn ways to manipulate the compatibility of your roles, this will permit you to influence the ease with which you can move into the parent role. The skills that permit this are: (1) knowing what role compatibility is, (2) being able to recognize it in your own life situation, and (3) being able to consciously change the compatibility of your roles. Some examples of things that can be done to increase the compatibility of the parent role with other roles are:

1. *Compartmentalize roles*. This means to separate the time and place of one's various roles. For example, if the parenthood role is incompatible with the creative artist role, it might help to move the art studio out of the house and confine time for art when one doesn't have parental duties.

2. *Change expectations.* You could change some of your beliefs about what you or someone else ought to do in one or several roles. Perhaps you are too demanding or rigid, and "giving in" would help eliminate the role incompatibility.

3. *Eliminate a role*. Sometimes you could quit doing something, such as participating in a sports club, being a volunteer, or working on a job.

4. *Rearrange obligations.* Sometimes spouses could rearrange their tasks to eliminate role incompatibilities. Many couples have both husband and wife share in various household and child care responsibilities, and another strategy is to divide the tasks in unorthodox ways.

In this chapter you have learned about preparing for parenthood. By applying the two principles above, you will become better, more responsible, and more efficient as a parent.

Chapter 6: Your Marriage as the Years Pass

A number of studies were conducted in the past decades in an attempt to discover what happens to spouses' feelings toward each other as they become parents and begin the process of raising their children. These studies have conclusively shown that the typical pattern is for love feelings to become less intense and for marriages to become less satisfying and less pleasant during the first 10 to 15 years. This is frequently followed by a period when marriages become somewhat more pleasant after the children are grown and leave home. These studies also found out that there is a pattern of gradual disillusionment, and couples can avoid this if they can learn what it takes to be among the minority who maintain or enhance their marital relationship. This last chapter identifies ways in which one of the principles discussed in an earlier chapter and another new principle can help couples attain this goal.

Principles of Enriching Marriage as the Years Pass

One principle that seems very relevant in this context is the *Interaction Principle* discussed in the first chapter. One reason this principle seems to be important in maintaining a satisfactory, long-term marital relationship is the observable pattern in most marriages that the couple spends less and less time interacting. These neglected activities include sharing precious moments, talking about their days, going out together, and in general, being close companions and friends. As the children come, and the husband and wife become increasingly involved in careers, housekeeping, community service, individual leisure activities, etc., couples usually find their interaction as companions tends to decrease.

You can use the Interaction Principle to manipulate your situations so that you can maintain the level of positive feelings (love) toward each other that you wish. The steps to this are: (1) to determine profitable ways in which you can interact; (2) to maintain an optimal level of such profitable interaction; (3) to decrease unprofitable interaction as much as possible; and (4) to increase the interaction in the profit you have. Two exercises of this principle in chapter one deal with these ways to implement this principle. If you are interested in these issues, you may wish to revisit those exercises or invent some of your own.

It has been said that the successful marriage is not so much avoiding problems as it is dealing with problems encountered in ways that create success. All couples face a countless number of problems. However, if you and your partner learn how to communicate with each other in comfortable, open, and reassuring ways, the two of you have a skill that will go a long way toward helping you maintain and enrich your marital relationship.

THE JOINT INVOLVEMENT PRINCIPLE:

> The more spouses are jointly involved in their social networks, the more similar the spouses will become, and vice versa.

We're not talking about social networking sites here. These social networks include relatives, friendship groups, work groups, social groups, social clubs, and service organizations.

Two skills are involved in using this principle. The first is being able to recognize which social groups you and your spouse belong to and to recognize how those groups influence the two of you. As your attitudes, beliefs, values, hopes, dreams, and goals gradually change, the groups always seem to change. In fact, what seems to occur is that, if you aren't comfortable with the groups you have identified with, you change the groups so that you can interact comfortably, and then the new groups influence you. It takes some skill, however, to recognize what these groups are and how they bring about gradual changes in yourself and your spouse.

The second skill that you need in order to use this principle is to be able to actively do something about these groups. Many of us become involved with different groups at different stages of our adult life. For example, we may be very involved at one stage of our life with groups that are active participants in sporting events, such as car racing, collegiate athletics, beachcombing, or horse racing, but this involvement may last only a few years. Many of us find ourselves participating in groups such as these until we buy a house, have children, and adopt a quieter lifestyle. When these latter events occur, we find that the groups we are involved with change. As this change occurs, it becomes possible to actively plan and direct some of our activities.

One very common pattern among couples is for the husband to become highly involved in his career and out-of-family activities, for the wife to become involved in her motherly and home-oriented concerns, and for both them to become integrated with different groups. One way of changing this pattern is for the husband to become more involved in the home by spending more time there and by assuming more responsibilities for the supervision of the children, the care of the home, and household tasks. At the same time, the wife can become more involved in out-of-family concerns and groups by giving more emphasis to a career, service activities, artistic creativity, her education, etc. One of the beauties of contemporary society is that the rigid definitions of what husbands and wives ought to do have now become flexible enough to give most of us considerable freedom in the way we structure our activities.

In addition to the two principles mentioned above, there are many other principles that can be used to maintain and enhance your marital relationship as the years pass. For example, you can use the principles on how to change your marital ties and the principles about love, so your marriage will be able to stand the test of time.

Conclusion

Thank you again for purchasing this book!

I hope this book helped you learn the core principles of successful marriages and how to apply them to your situation.

The next step is to try to talk with your spouse about how to implement these principles to start improving your marriage.

Thank you and good luck!